HEADS UP!
CONCUSSION
AWARENESS

SIMON ROSE

CRABTREE
Publishing Company
www.crabtreebooks.com

CRABTREE
PUBLISHING COMPANY
WWW.CRABTREEBOOKS.COM

Author: Simon Rose

Series Research and Development: Reagan Miller

Editors: Janine Deschenes, Kenneth Lane

Proofreader: Wendy Scavuzzo

Design: Margaret Amy Salter

Photo research: Margaret Amy Salter

Production coordinator and
  Prepress technician: Margaret Amy Salter, Abigail Smith

Print coordinator: Katherine Berti

Consultant: Kenneth Lane, Bioscientist and Science Writer and Editor

Photo Credits
t=Top, tr=Top Right, tl=Top Left, br=bottom right,

Shutterstock: ©Julia Baturina pp 6-7 (t),
©Jakkrit Orrasri p 9 (br), ©Alexander Ishchenko p 16 (l),
©Aspen Photo p 28 (tl), ©StockphotoVideo p 30,
©Richard Thornton p 40 (br), ©Maxisport p 40 (l)

Dartmouth College: Eli Burakian p 43

iStock: KatarzynaBialasiewicz p 35 (tr)

Wikimedia: p 33 public domaine s(tr)

All other images from Shutterstock

Library and Archives Canada Cataloguing in Publication

Rose, Simon, 1961- author
        Heads up! : concussion awareness / Simon Rose

(Exploring the brain)
Includes bibliographical references and index.
Issued in print and electronic formats.
ISBN 978-0-7787-3508-3 (hardcover).--
ISBN 978-0-7787-3512-0 (softcover).--
ISBN 978-1-4271-1996-4 (HTML)

        1. Brain--Concussion--Juvenile literature. 2. Head--Wounds and
injuries--Juvenile literature. I. Title.

RC394.C7R57 2017   j617.4'81044   C2017-906551-3
                                                C2017-906552-1

Library of Congress Cataloging-in-Publication Data

Names: Rose, Simon, 1961- author.
Title: Heads up! : concussion awareness / Simon Rose.
Description: New York, New York : Crabtree Publishing Company,
  [2018] | Series: Exploring the brain | Includes bibliographical
  references and index.
Identifiers: LCCN 2017059663 (print) | LCCN 2017060176 (ebook) |
  ISBN 9781427119964 (Electronic HTML) |
  ISBN 9780778735083 (reinforced library binding) |
  ISBN 9780778735120 (pbk.)
Subjects: LCSH: Brain--Concussion--Juvenile literature. |
  Brain--Wounds and injuries--Juvenile literature. |
  Sports injuries--Juvenile literature.
Classification: LCC RC394.C7 (ebook) | LCC RC394.C7 R67 2018
  (print) | DDC 617.4/81044--dc23
LC record available at https://lccn.loc.gov/2017059663

Crabtree Publishing Company

www.crabtreebooks.com   1-800-387-7650

Printed in the U.S.A./022018/CG20171220

Published in Canada
Crabtree Publishing
616 Welland Ave.
St. Catharines, Ontario
L2M 5V6

Published in the United States
Crabtree Publishing
PMB 59051
350 Fifth Avenue, 59th Floor
New York, New York 10118

Published in the United Kingdom
Crabtree Publishing
Maritime House
Basin Road North, Hove
BN41 1WR

Published in Australia
Crabtree Publishing
3 Charles Street
Coburg North
VIC, 3058

Table of Contents

CHAPTER 1

What Is a CONCUSSION?

The human brain plays a vital part in everything that we do. It is connected to the spinal cord to make up the body's central nervous system. The brain has two sides. The right half looks after the left side of the body. The left half of the brain is responsible for the body's right side.

Your brain helps you remember everyday things, such as how to type on a keyboard.

The brain works as the human body's control center. It controls important things such as our breathing and heartbeat. The brain also helps us organize our thoughts, and remember how to do things. It helps us decide to act in a certain way, such as when we are walking, eating, or grabbing something with our fingers. The brain allows us to think and process, or understand, information that comes from our senses. This helps us make sense of the world around us, and also helps us recognize dangerous situations in which we might get hurt.

Different parts of the brain look after our senses and language. The brain also helps us remember how to do things we've done before. This includes things such as writing, swimming, cycling, the rules of a game, or other things in our daily lives.

The important parts of the human body are protected from injury. The ribcage protects the vital, or important, organs in our chest and upper body, such as our heart and lungs.

skull

rib cage

The skull protects the brain. The top of the skull is called the **cranium**. There, the bones are joined together to protect the brain. The brain is also protected by fluid that surrounds the brain inside the skull.

Besides the cranium, other bones in the skull protect the brain. There are bones where the eyes, nose, and mouth are located. There are also bones inside the ear. The brain is well protected for good reason. If it gets damaged, there can be serious consequences. This book helps you learn about one of the most common brain injuries, and how you can take control of your brain health to avoid it!

If you hit your head hard enough, your brain might collide with one of the many bones in your skull.

Nathan's Story

Although the brain is very well protected, it can still be damaged. One of the most common brain injuries is called a concussion. This is also known as a **mild traumatic brain injury or mTBI**. A concussion can happen any time the head suffers an impact. It can happen when falling off a bike, playing, or when bumping into objects or into other people. A concussion can cause problems with our vision, balance, speech, and concentration, and lead to headaches. Concussions are often not obvious right away. Sometimes, they are only discovered after a visit to the doctor or to a hospital.

Want to learn more about concussions and the effects they can have on us? Let's get started by hearing Nathan's story.

Nathan Fraser was only 12 years old when he suffered a concussion during hockey practice in early 2012. Nathan was playing as the defenseman during a two-on-one drill. When one of the forwards missed a pass from one of his teammates, he skated after the puck. Nathan chased after him toward the boards. When the forward dived for the puck, Nathan collided with him. Nathan went head first into the boards. He also banged his head on the ice.

He was unconscious for almost one minute. When Nathan woke up, the coach asked him questions to see whether he might have experienced a concussion. Nathan lay on the ice for about ten minutes before he was taken to the nearest hospital.

"The next thing I remember is being at the hospital," said Nathan. "My memory is foggy, but I know I was in a room with a doctor and he was asking me questions, doing tests with a pen to check my vision, and checking how strong I was. Afterwards he said I had a pretty bad concussion and then he let me go home."

At first, Nathan had headaches and **nausea**, and was often dizzy and off balance. A few days after the accident, Nathan also became more sensitive to sound and light. He had to wear sunglasses and earmuffs most of the time. Some sounds, such as barking dogs, made him cry because his ears hurt so much. He could only watch TV if he faced away from it a little with the volume very low. A few days after the accident, he began to **slur** his speech. He also had weak arms and legs, and was always tired.

Nathan was away from school for almost five months. His friends and classmates didn't really understand what had happened to him. Like most kids, they didn't know how serious it could be to hurt their head. Nathan's recovery took a while, but eventually he even returned to hockey.

Nathan suffered a concussion as a sports injury, but a concussion can happen to anyone. Luckily, the people around Nathan recognized that his accident might have caused a concussion. He was then able to get the proper treatment to help him recover.

Every story of a concussion experience is different, and Nathan's is just one of them. To make sure you don't experience a similar injury, read on to learn more about what a concussion is, its effects, and how it can be treated.

So, What Are Concussions?

A concussion, or mild traumatic brain injury (mTBI) is an injury to the brain. It is referred to as mild because concussions are not usually life threatening. However, concussions have serious effects and can change how the brain works.

The brain is cushioned, or protected, by fluid, and the skull shields the brain like a helmet. But if the head is hit hard enough, the brain can be damaged. A blow or impact can make the head move back and forth quickly. This can make the brain move around inside the skull. The brain might bang against the skull bones, which can damage brain **cells**, or cause **chemical** changes inside the brain.

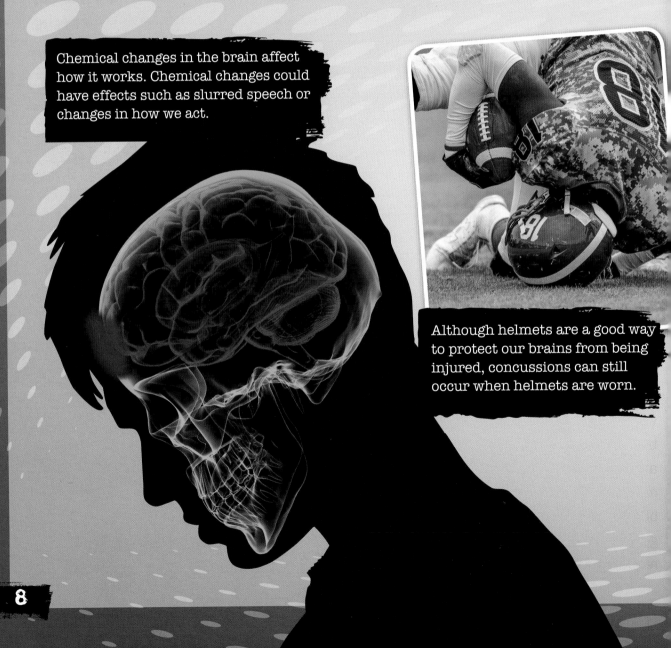

Chemical changes in the brain affect how it works. Chemical changes could have effects such as slurred speech or changes in how we act.

Although helmets are a good way to protect our brains from being injured, concussions can still occur when helmets are worn.

When we are injured, there are usually signs that we are hurt. There are cuts, bruises, and perhaps swelling in the injured area. This helps doctors see where the injury is located and show them how to treat it. When the brain is injured, we may have bruises or cuts on our head or face, but we cannot see signs of injury on the brain. However, an injury to the brain can be far more serious than a broken bone, sprain, or cut.

On the surface, nothing may seem to be wrong after a concussion. However, a concussion can affect things such as how we see, hear, talk, and move. The brain controls everything that the body does. This means that any damage to the brain can cause all kinds of problems in different parts of the body.

The brain's **temporal lobe** processes memories. If it is damaged, the person may not remember the accident that caused their concussion.

When we think of a head injury, we often think of a person becoming **unconscious**. But a person doesn't have to fall unconscious if they suffer from a concussion. Some people do, then they forget what happened before they were injured because their memory has been affected. Other people who have a concussion may remain awake and remember everything. Recovery times can be different. Some concussion victims may get better after a few weeks. Others may recover in only a few hours.

Many sports players have experienced concussions. They may or may not fall unconscious.

9

CONCUSSION FACTS

There are **50 TBI** hospitalizations in Canada every day. Many of these are older people who have suffered falls. The number of people treated for these types of injuries will increase as the population of the country ages.

1 in 5 sports injuries are concussions.

There are **3.8 million** concussions in the United States every year as a result of sports and recreation.

Sports- and recreation-related injuries account for **64%** of visits to emergency departments by 10 to 18 year olds.

EMERGENCY

More than **90%** of concussions do not result in the person becoming unconscious, so it can be difficult to tell if they have a concussion.

In the United States in 2012,

329,290

children and teens aged 19 or younger treated in emergency departments for sports- or recreation-related injuries were **diagnosed** with a concussion or traumatic brain injury.

Around **50%** of concussions are never reported. This is the case for a number of reasons, such as people not realizing they have a serious injury or when athletes do not want to admit that they might be hurt.

THINK ABOUT IT!

How is a concussion different from an injury to another part of the body, such as a broken arm or leg? In what ways are these injuries the same?

CHAPTER 2

CAUSES,
Signs, and Symptoms

As we've learned, most concussions are caused by a hard blow to the head. The injured person experiences pain on the outside of their head as a result of the injury. There might also be cuts, bruises, or swelling on the head, neck, or face. However, depending on how severe the concussion is, the real damage is inside the skull.

In the image below, the **paramedic** can see a cut on the outside of the person's head. This suggests to the paramedic that the person has had a head injury, and could have a concussion. But sometimes, there are little or no signs of a head injury or concussion.

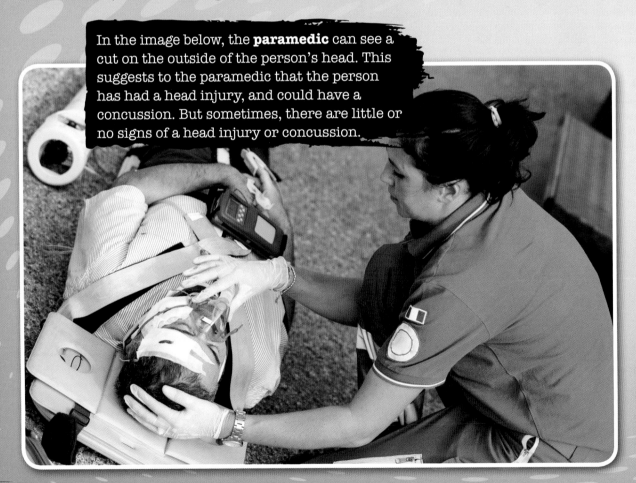

What Happens to the Brain During a Concussion?

Your skull, and the fluid that surrounds your brain, is meant to take most of the impact of a hit. The fluid goes back and forth inside the skull, moving the brain at the same time. If there is a very hard impact, the brain can also bang against the bone inside the skull. This impact can cause the **brain tissue** to bruise or change shape, and brain cells to stretch.

Damage to brain cells makes it more difficult for them to do what they're supposed to. If the damaged cells control our vision, we will not be able to see properly. If the damaged cells are those that are connected to speech and language, the damage to them will affect how we can speak. In some concussions, the body's systems might not work properly for only a few minutes, then go back to normal. In other concussions, the brain damage might last for months or even years. Some people never fully recover.

neuron, a type of brain cell

fluid

skull

ELECTRIC BODY

The nervous system is a little like electrical wiring. Imagine looking at a very confusing collection of electrical wires and cables, perhaps in lots of different colors. These wires and cables are connected to a main control area. This control area is your central nervous system. Each wire or cable has a job to do. Many of the wires and cables might also be connected to each other. The wires and cables make up your **peripheral nervous system**. The central and peripheral nervous systems work together to make up your nervous system. Damage in one area can affect how the whole system operates.

peripheral nervous system

central nervous system

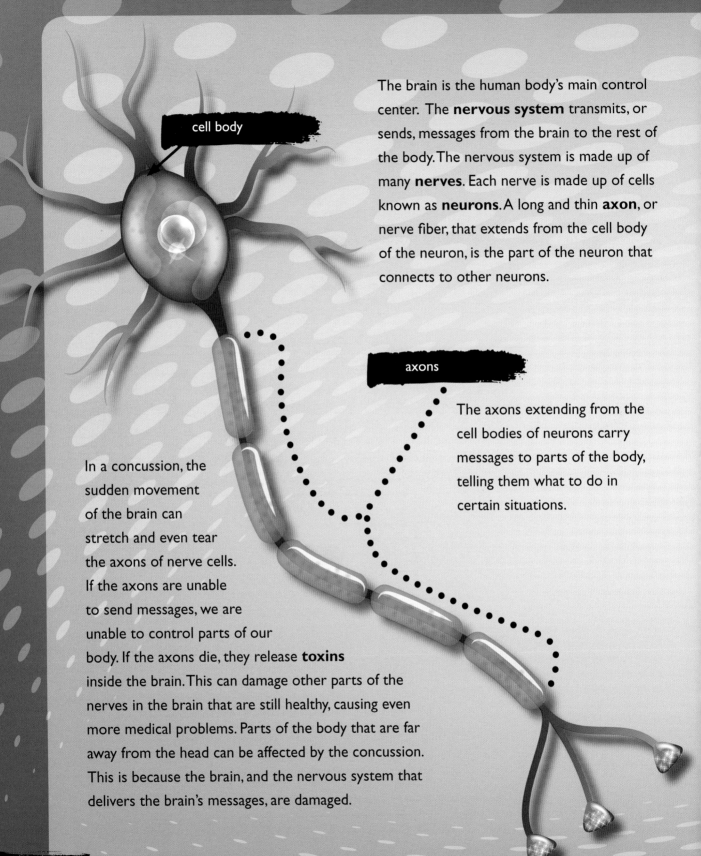

cell body

The brain is the human body's main control center. The **nervous system** transmits, or sends, messages from the brain to the rest of the body. The nervous system is made up of many **nerves**. Each nerve is made up of cells known as **neurons**. A long and thin **axon**, or nerve fiber, that extends from the cell body of the neuron, is the part of the neuron that connects to other neurons.

axons

The axons extending from the cell bodies of neurons carry messages to parts of the body, telling them what to do in certain situations.

In a concussion, the sudden movement of the brain can stretch and even tear the axons of nerve cells. If the axons are unable to send messages, we are unable to control parts of our body. If the axons die, they release **toxins** inside the brain. This can damage other parts of the nerves in the brain that are still healthy, causing even more medical problems. Parts of the body that are far away from the head can be affected by the concussion. This is because the brain, and the nervous system that delivers the brain's messages, are damaged.

In the National Football League (NFL), the most common causes of concussions among football players are from impacts next to the ear or between the eyes. This kind of blow causes the brain to rock back and forth. When the head is hit hard enough, the brain hits against the inside of the skull several times. The worst kind of concussion that a football player can have is called a rotational concussion. The impact in this type of concussion causes the brain to spin and twist inside the skull's fluid. It does this in the opposite direction to where the player was hit. The brain moves from side to side as well as forward and backward. This stretches and spins the nerve fibers. Some of them might even break. **Blood vessels** in the brain might also be damaged or break. The vessels then bleed inside the brain. If blood vessels bleed into the brain tissue, the bleeding can kill neurons.

first impact

second impact

BRAIN LAB

PROTECT THE EGG

Complete an exercise to help you understand how brain injuries can happen and how our skulls protect us. Take a glass jar and fill it halfway with water. Then place a raw egg in the water. The jar represents the skull, the egg the brain, and the water the fluid surrounding the brain. Make sure that the jar's lid is fastened tightly then move the jar slightly. This shows how the brain moves around inside the skull, protected by the fluid.

Next, shake the jar containing the water and the egg as hard as you can. This will show you how the brain can be hurt when you suffer a hard blow to your head. What happens to the egg inside the jar?

Concussion Causes

In sports, concussions happen for many different reasons. A sudden blow to the head from impact with another player or with a piece of sports equipment causes the head to snap sideways, forward, or backward. A blow to the player's body can cause similar head movement and make the head collide with another person, a wall, or the playing surface. A player might trip or fall without anyone else being involved, causing the head to hit a hard surface. A concussion might also happen even if the head isn't hit directly. An impact somewhere else on the body might cause a **whiplash** movement. This causes the person's head to snap toward the location of the impact and to then spin in the opposite direction.

Sports with a high risk of concussions include **hockey, football, soccer, rugby, and boxing.** Other recreational activities with a risk of head injuries include **skiing, snowboarding, horseback riding, skateboarding, cycling, and rollerblading.**

1 in 5 high school athletes will suffer a concussion during the season in which they are active in their sport.

High school football is the cause of **47%** of all concussions caused during sports.

Soccer has the most concussions for girls' sports.

20% of all skiing and snowboarding injuries involve severe head trauma.

Concussions do not only happen in contact sports. Car accidents and falls are the most common causes of concussions in adults. Car accidents—even small ones such as being rear-ended at a stop sign—often cause whiplash, which can result in a concussion. A concussion might also result from a bicycle accident. Falls can cause damage to the head and brain, and are most likely to occur in young children and older adults.

Children sometimes hurt themselves when playing. Older adults are more likely to be unsteady on their feet or suffer from dizzy spells that cause them to stumble and trip, sometimes falling and banging their head. Head injuries are always a possibility when people rush and have accidents or when people fight. Soldiers in combat situations or law enforcement officers are also often in dangerous situations where a concussion could happen.

People who have already had a concussion are more likely to have a second one. This is because the brain may not have fully recovered from the first concussion.

More than **500,000** people visit emergency rooms in the United States every year for injuries related to cycling. Bike helmets reduce the risk of head injury by **45%.**

18% of horseback riding injuries are head injuries.

THINK ABOUT IT!

Concussions are not only sport injuries. What other kinds of situations might lead to a person suffering a concussion?

Identifying the Signs and Symptoms of a Concussion

If a person suffers a blow to the head, there are a number of ways to check if they may have a concussion. They might immediately show signs of having a concussion. But it could also be hours or several days before anyone notices anything unusual about someone who has had a concussion. Some **symptoms** last for hours or days, and others for a number of weeks or even months. After an accident, a person who has suffered a concussion might be unconscious. If they have external injuries such as cuts or bruises on the head or face, or have fluid or blood coming from the nose or ears, they may have a concussion. In these cases, they should be checked after they are awake to see if they have a concussion. But people do not have to lose consciousness to have a concussion. In fact, most people with a concussion stay awake.

A person who may have a concussion should receive medical attention from a doctor or at a hospital as soon as possible.

Concussions can affect a range of body functions and cause many different symptoms. Read below to learn about some of the signs of a concussion.

A concussed person might have a bad headache that keeps getting worse, and lasts for more than a few minutes.

Someone with a concussion might suffer from nausea, which means that they feel like throwing up.

Concussions can cause blurred vision and other vision problems, or sensitivity to light and noise.

Confusion is a common symptom of concussion. The person might not understand where they are, or what happened. A person suffering a concussion might also be unable to concentrate, make decisions, or answer questions.

They could have a ringing sound in the ears or problems with their sense of taste or smell.

Their speech might be slurred, or they may say things that don't make sense.

The person could have trouble with their balance, feel dizzy, and find it difficult to walk.

Friends and family might notice personality changes in someone who has had a concussion. The person who was injured may feel sleepy or restless. They may also feel extreme emotions, such as anger or sadness, for no reason. Concussions can also affect a person's memory. Some people who have had a concussion do not remember the accident that caused the concussion. At other times, the concussion can cause a loss of memory of everything that happened before the concussion.

Concussions can be more difficult to recognize in very young children. Unlike adults, young children are not always able to answer questions about how they feel. Head injuries often happen to young children and the symptoms are similar to those in adults. Other signs of a concussion in young children include getting tired easily or crying much more than usual. There might be changes in sleep or eating habits, or a lack of interest in what used to be favorite activities or toys.

THINK ABOUT IT!

A concussion is not always an obvious injury since there are usually no noticeable signs of it. Think about how other injuries are diagnosed by doctors and medical professionals. For example, what are the signs that an arm is broken? Now imagine you are trying to recognize if your friend might have a concussion. What questions might you ask them? What behaviors might you look for?

Diagnosing a Concussion

Diagnosing a concussion as soon as possible is important. An undiagnosed concussion can lead to brain damage, causing problems such as frequent headaches, trouble concentrating, and **seizures**. Getting the proper treatment quickly after a head injury will help the recovery from a concussion. If you have a head or neck injury, a doctor will ask you how you are feeling and how your injury happened. They will ask you if you have any of the symptoms that are usually caused by a concussion. The doctor might ask you to go through some tests to check if your memory is working properly. These involve simple questions such as your name, address, your family members, or what day of the week it is. Other tests can check your nerves, balance, and **reflexes**.

A doctor might decide to look at your brain with a **CT** or **CAT scan** (above), or an **MRI scan** (below). These scans help the doctor to examine the brain without having to perform surgery to see inside the body. They will then be able to decide what treatment is needed.

BRAIN LAB

This game using numbers helps you to understand how a concussion might affect a person's memory. You will need to do the exercise with a partner.

For the first exercise, read out the following numbers to your partner. Read the numbers one at a time. When you have finished, your partner can write the numbers down and read them back to you. How many did they get correct?

8567

78982

299698

3942190

In the second exercise, you will read the numbers in chunks. For example, you will say 8 5 6 7 as "eighty-five," "sixty-seven." Once again, have your partner write the numbers down, then read them back to you, after you are finished. How did they do this time?

You can swap places, with your partner reading the numbers and you writing them down.

When you and your partner have both completed the exercises, talk about which exercise was more difficult. The first exercise should show you the limits of short-term memory. Memory loss is a common symptom of concussion. These exercises show you how serious a concussion can be if it prevents you from remembering a simple set of numbers correctly.

Esther's Story

Some people recover from a concussion in a few hours and others in a few weeks. Although people who have concussions improve afterward, concussions can also have both short-term and long-term effects.

"Before my concussion in eighth grade," said Esther, *"I played soccer, hockey, and tennis, I was a dedicated student, and life was good. I experienced the concussion during a soccer game, and did not know enough to take myself out of the game despite dizziness, nausea, blurry vision, and confusion. It took me a long time to realize that this was serious. I had no idea that this seemingly harmless hit would turn my life upside down."*

Esther Lovett first suffered a concussion when playing soccer in grade eight. She then suffered another concussion before her junior year of high school. In between her accidents, she had **post-concussion syndrome (PCS)** for more than two years.

Post-concussion syndrome means that symptoms of a concussion last for more than four weeks. The symptoms can be worse if the person has suffered a previous concussion or head injury, or if they have had a headache after their injury. More than 30 percent of concussion patients have post-concussion syndrome. At first, Esther just wanted to go back to playing soccer, but she had many signs that she had a concussion. In math class, the numbers on the board would become so blurred to her eyes that she got severe headaches and had to leave the classroom. Before her accident, she loved math class and was often a step ahead of her classmates. She also liked watching documentaries in history class. But after her accident, she found it too uncomfortable. Looking at the screen caused a headache and nausea. She always had to leave the room. At lunch time, the noise around her made it difficult for her to concentrate. Esther also had trouble keeping track of her friends' conversations.

Esther later realized that she had to give up contact sports. This was a difficult decision, since she had been playing soccer for years. However, Esther decided to learn a new sport and started to play golf. This helped her to get her life back on track and to recover from her concussion. In tenth grade, Esther was asked by the Boston Children's Hospital to do a television interview about concussions and the Children's Brain Injury Center. This helped to raise awareness about children and teenagers who had suffered from concussions.

CONCUSSION
Legacy Foundation

Just before her junior year of high school, Esther fell down some stairs and suffered another concussion. This time, her symptoms were worse and she could not continue at school. Although Esther recovered from her injury, it had long-term effects and her PCS changed her life. Since she could no longer study, Esther decided that she would dedicate herself to concussion awareness, helping others who have been injured and educating people about concussions. Esther worked as an intern at the Concussion Legacy Foundation. She also worked with the Boston Children's Hospital.

CHAPTER 3

TREATMENT and RECOVERY

Most concussions can be treated if they are diagnosed right away. Suppose you are riding your bike when you have a nasty fall and hit your head. Even though you are wearing a helmet, you have an instant headache and feel confused, dizzy, and nauseous. Your parents take you to the hospital. There, a doctor will ask which symptoms are the most painful. The doctor might also ask if any symptoms get worse in certain situations, such as when you are exposed to loud sounds or bright lights. You are diagnosed with a concussion.

It is important to see a doctor if you think you might have a concussion, and to recommend this to someone else who might have one. A doctor can help guide your recovery.

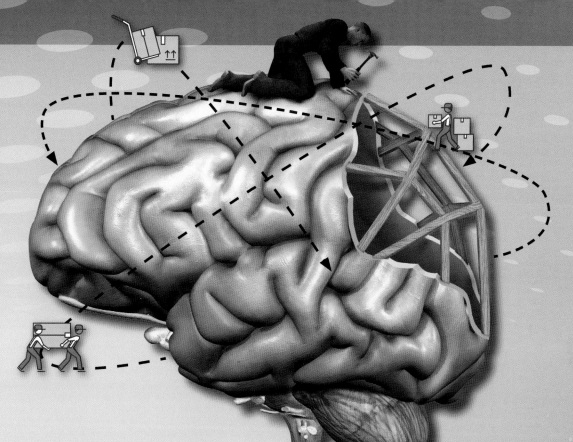

The doctor will then recommend what you should do to recover (read more on the next page!), and when you should gradually return to your normal activities. Most people recover after a concussion. How quickly they recover depends on how severe their concussion is, their health before the injury, their age, and how they behave after the injury. Communication is also an important part of the recovery process. You need to talk to your doctor, parents, teachers, or coaches about how you feel physically, in your mind, and emotionally. Talking about how you feel can help you recover from your concussion.

The brain is able to reorganize itself as we learn new things during our lifetime. This process is called **neuroplasticity**. It can also help the brain recover after an injury. Using the process of neuroplasticity, a healthy part of the brain can take over the work previously done by a part of the brain that was damaged. We referred earlier to the nervous system being like wiring or cables. Neuroplasticity is almost like rewiring or rearranging the cables within a damaged part of the nervous system. It is a complicated process that needs time to work properly. That's why it is so important to take your recovery seriously.

The Right Recovery

Rest is very important when recovering from a concussion. You need to get plenty of rest in the daytime and plenty of sleep at night. If you are able to go to school, your doctor might recommend taking more breaks, having shorter days, and doing less schoolwork while you are recovering. At first, you will need to stop using computers, playing video games, texting on your phone, or watching television. The screens and the need to concentrate when doing these activities are likely to give you a headache. You should also avoid heavy physical activity, strenuous exercise, and any sports until you are feeling better. Since you may have trouble concentrating, you should also avoid riding a bicycle or using such things as household appliances or tools.

Crowds and places where there might be loud noises or bright lights might make you feel worse.

If something makes your symptoms worse or you start to have new symptoms, stop doing that activity and talk to your doctor. As you get better, you will be able to gradually spend more time on your favorite activities, be at school more often, and do more homework and assignments. Once all the symptoms of your concussion have disappeared, your doctor will let you know when you can go back to your usual daily activities.

During your recovery, your doctor may give you some medicine for your pain. You can take some kinds of **pain relievers** for headaches, but should always check with your doctor first. You should not take any other medicines unless your doctor tells you that it is okay to do so.

Concussion symptoms often last for only seven to ten days. However, it usually takes longer for the brain to fully recover. Because of this, it is important to take things slowly in recovery. Limit your time when using computers, watching television, playing games, or meeting your friends. It is normal to feel frustrated that you are unable to return to your regular life as quickly as you would like. If you try to rush your recovery, you could make it even longer!

People who suffer from post-concussion syndrome need to be especially careful to avoid situations that may cause another concussion. Second-impact syndrome happens when someone suffers a second concussion before recovering from a first one. This can be very dangerous and cause swelling in the brain. Some athletes have died from a second concussion. This often happens because the first one was never diagnosed. An athlete who has had more than one concussion while playing or practicing needs to think about permanently leaving that sport.

THINK ABOUT IT!

Imagine that you have suffered a concussion. What kinds of activities that you normally do would you have to temporarily give up as you recover? What kinds of things might you do instead that would help you to get better more quickly?

Gender and Concussions

Although concussions can happen to anyone, recent medical studies have shown that they can be different for females than for males. Concussions in females can also often be worse than in males. Females can also take longer to recover. This is true even when boys and girls participate in the same sport with the same rules, such as soccer, baseball, or basketball.

Until recently, most research into concussions has been done on adult male athletes who have been injured. This is because male athletes usually play more contact sports and so are more likely to be injured. However, recent research by the American Osteopathic Association on boys and girls aged 11 to 18 in middle school and high school shows that the girls might take more than twice as long as the boys to recover from a concussion. A study of medical records showed that concussion symptoms lasted for around 11 days in the average boy, and for 28 days in the average girl.

There are many differences between male and female brains. The most obvious difference between the brains of men and women is overall size—men's brains are, on average, between 10 and 15 percent larger than women's. In females, the part of the brain controlling memory is larger. This means that they absorb more information from their emotions and senses than males do. The left and right sides of the female brain also communicate with each other more than they do in males.

Because of these and other differences, it makes sense that injuries to the brain would be different in girls than they are in boys. Differences in the damage caused by a concussion can also be due to medical conditions that existed in someone before the concussion occurs. Some types of mental conditions, such as **anxiety**, and bad headaches called **migraines** are more common in young females than they are in males. When a concussion happens, these things might make the symptoms of the concussion last longer, or might make them worse in females.

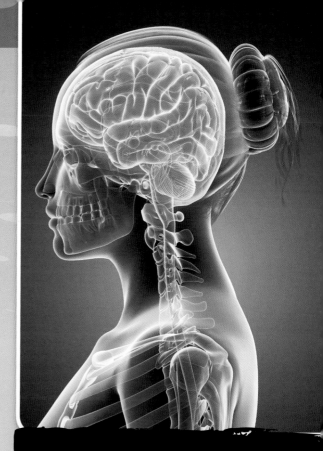

Female athletes may also have more concussions, depending on the strength of their neck and the size of their head. Women tend to have smaller heads and more slender necks than men.

PINK Concussion

PINK Concussions is a non-profit organization that hopes to improve education about concussions in women and girls, including their treatment and recovery from them. The organization works with women and girls who have brain injuries from sports, military service, accidents, or violence. PINK Concussions organizes international conferences where brain injury experts can share and discuss information and new research. In 2016, the organization held two international summits, or conferences. PINK Concussions has online communities to help support young women who are isolated by a concussion. It has created online support groups and educational resources for schools, medical clinics, and sports organizations.

Simran's Story

For some people, the long-term recovery from a concussion can change their lives forever. There can be many challenges during the recovery process. It is very important that people who have had concussions look after themselves and follow their doctor's instructions about treatment. People who are injured also need the support of their family and friends.

In 2016, Simran Kohli suffered a concussion during water polo practice. She had a very bad headache and nausea, and was very dizzy. At first, she did not realize that she was seriously injured. But the following week at school Simran couldn't focus in class, saw words as jumbled, and could only look at a screen for a few minutes. Once she knew something was wrong, she took time off from school to try to get better. She spent a lot of time in her room with the curtains drawn, avoiding bright light. She slept a lot. Her headache made her feel like throwing up and she often didn't feel like eating. Even in the house, she wore a hoodie, hat, and sunglasses. She only went outside to go to doctor's appointments. She just wanted to go back to school but no one could tell her how long she would need to get better. She had very little contact with her friends, teammates, or coach. They knew she was hurt but not how serious it was.

Simran did go back to school after three weeks, but the noise and lights that were part of the school day made her headache worse. She also had little support from classmates. Because Simran had no outward signs of injury, her classmates and other people assumed that she was fine. They didn't understand how she could be back at school if she was still concussed. They also didn't understand why she wasn't back on the water polo team.

Simran's family was a great help. They encouraged her to stay positive and focus on getting better. This helped Simran to slowly ease back into her studies, going to school part time, having less homework, and taking more time for tests. She had a constant headache for six months, but eventually recovered.

"Looking back," says Simran, *"I realize that the physical limitations from a concussion are difficult but they are emotionally compounded if you don't have support from your friends."*

In the quote (left), Simran describes how difficult it was for her to recover without support from her friends. If you have a friend who has suffered a concussion, reach out to them and offer a kind ear or helping hand.

CHAPTER 4

PROTECT
Yourself!

Concussions usually happen as a result of accidents. This makes them very hard to prevent. However, you can reduce the risk of a concussion happening to you and others using both your thoughts and your actions. Good decisions about personal safety and injury prevention can reduce the risk of a brain injury, in all situations.

Reducing the Risk

We have already seen how some contact sports make concussions more likely. Skateboarding, hockey, boxing, football, snowboarding, horseback riding, rollerblading, and cycling have high risks of injury. These sports often involve using a lot of equipment, a sometimes-dangerous environment, and playing at high speeds. In sports like these, protective equipment, such as helmets, padding, eye and mouth guards, can help prevent injury. For example, if a cyclist is involved in an accident, the risk of a severe head injury is reduced by 85 percent if a helmet is worn.

All protective equipment must fit properly, be kept in good condition, and be checked regularly. If protective equipment is damaged, it should not be used and should be thrown away.

In the United States, the American Society for Testing and Materials (ASTM) conducts safety tests before sports helmets are approved. If the helmet passes the test, it has an ASTM sticker. The Canadian Standards Association, now known as the CSA Group, carries out this work in Canada. People can then buy the helmet or other protective gear and feel confident that it will keep them safe.

The outer shell should be fully intact with no cracks, or dents in its surface.

Check the fit of the helmet. It should be snug on your head and sit low on your forehead, no more than two finger widths above your eyebrows. The strap should fit snugly under your chin.

Inner styrofoam should be undamaged. Check that there are no cracked or crushed parts.

The Y of the side straps should meet just below your ear. The buckle should be under your chin. The straps should not be worn or faded.

Buckle should not be damaged. Check for missing pieces or cracks.

Helmets and other protective headgear are available in many sizes. The equipment must fit properly if it is to offer the best protection. You must also wear the right helmet for the sport in which you are participating. For example, a bike helmet should not be worn for skating or hockey.

Helmets can protect a person from a fractured skull and other head injuries. However, remember that a concussion can still happen even if you are wearing a helmet. This is because an impact to the head causes the brain to move around inside the skull, rather than causing an injury to the outside of the head.

headgear

Car accidents are a major cause of concussions. A seat belt should be worn by anyone driving or riding as a passenger in a vehicle. This can help prevent hitting one's head against the hard parts inside a car. Child seats and booster seats for younger children must also be used properly in cars. Protective headgear should always be worn when riding a motorcycle, all-terrain vehicle, or snowmobile.

seat belts

NO DIVING

You can also reduce the possibility of a concussion by making a decision not to take risks. Never jump or dive into unknown water, since you do not know what is below the surface. At swimming pools and water parks, always follow all the posted safety instructions. Pools have hard surfaces and the floors around pools or other areas near water are usually slippery. This increases the risk of a fall resulting in a head injury from running or not walking carefully by the side of the pool. Water parks also usually have concrete surfaces and sturdy metal equipment that can cause head injuries if you collide with them.

Concussions can occur in many everyday situations, but the risk of injury and concussion can be reduced. Elderly men and women are more likely to have falls than younger people. Homes can be made safer for seniors by having handrails on both sides of staircases. Nonslip mats can be placed in baths and showers, and grab bars can be placed in appropriate places in bathrooms. But trips and falls don't happen to elderly people only. You can avoid falling by wearing proper footwear when you go out of the house. For example, flip-flops should not be worn when cycling or running. Shoelaces should also always be tied so that they do not cause you to fall. At home, work, or school, you can remove things from the floor that you or someone else might trip over. Homes can also be fitted with more lights so that it's easier for people to spot tripping hazards.

Removing tripping hazards from the floor is one way you can help keep your home concussion-free.

Homes can be made safe for children by having safety gates at the bottom and top of staircases. Guards can also be fitted on windows to stop children from falling out of them. Playground areas can have sand or other softer material to reduce the risk of serious injuries from falls.

THINK ABOUT IT!

How safe is your home? What kinds of hazards are there in your home that might cause someone to have an accident? How can you take action to reduce the risk of someone falling in your home?

Protecting Yourself and Others

If you think that you, or someone you know, might have a concussion, talk to the nearest person you trust. Feeling unsteady, blurred vision, nausea, and a headache are the most common symptoms. But not all of the usual concussion symptoms may be present. A person might have slurred speech, not make sense then they speak, or feel confused. Other less common symptoms of a concussion include a larger **pupil** in one eye than the other, inability to recognize people or places, or feeling very drowsy. These are sometimes hard to spot in someone who has a concussion, but talking and asking questions can help you identify them.

If you think that someone has a concussion, stay with them and watch them closely for changes until help arrives. Make sure that they stop the athletic or other activity that caused their head injury, and do not move them if they are lying down. The Recognize, Report, Rest strategy below is a good way to make sure you are giving the right care to a person who might have a concussion.

Until help arrives, your coach, teacher, parents, or friends can help you identify symptoms and help take care of you or the person you think might have a concussion.

Recognize	Report	Rest
Now that you know some symptoms of concussions, recognize when a concussion may have occurred.	Let teachers, parents, coaches, or other adults know right away.	The concussed person should rest their brain to support recovery.

Making sure that your brain, nervous system, and body are healthy can help you recover from a concussion. Regular exercise is good for the body. Even the brain can be exercised by doing activities, such as puzzles, that make you think and concentrate.

You should drink at least eight glasses of water every day. It is best not to eat too much sugar or processed food, such as frozen pizza, salty snacks, or candy. The fats, salts, sugar, and other ingredients in processed foods can prevent the brain from learning or fighting disease, and can affect our memory. There are many foods that are good for your brain, though. See the chart below for some brain-friendly food options.

Vitamins are very good for brain health and are found in many foods. Vitamin C helps make the **neurotransmitters** of our nervous system. This helps the brain send and receive messages. Vitamin D helps with brain development, memory, and problem solving. The different kinds of Vitamin B help keep the brain and nervous system healthy as we age.

Vitamin B6

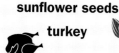

- avocado
- bananas
- chicken
- potatoes
- spinach
- sunflower seeds
- turkey

Vitamin B12

- beef
- lamb
- milk
- shrimp
- yogurt

Vitamin D

- beef
- liver
- cheese
- egg yolks

Vitamin C

- citrus fruits
- strawberries
- leafy greens
- bell peppers
- tomatoes

These vitamins are also in some types of fish, including cod, halibut, mackerel, salmon, sardines, and tuna. Vitamin D can be made in our bodies by sunlight striking our skin.

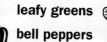

You can also share concussion awareness. You can educate others about the dangers of concussions, the need for protective sports equipment, removing everyday hazards for concussion, and ways to prevent concussions. You can give them tips about staying healthy and avoiding risks. If you know the symptoms of a concussion, you can help others recognize them. This could help others recognize symptoms of a concussion in themselves and in people they know or meet. It's also important to learn and share ways to support people who have had a concussion. Understand that even though they may look normal, they are still recovering. Support them in their recovery by modifying everyday activities with them, offering your help at school, or talking to them to try to understand how they are feeling. Try the Brain Lab on the next page with your peers at school or at home, to get more of an understanding of what the symptoms of a concussion feel like.

THINK ABOUT IT!

If you saw someone fall or experience an impact that might cause a head injury, what would you do? How would you know if they might have a concussion? What symptoms would you look for? What could you do to help them before medical help arrives?

BRAIN LAB

Concussion Stations

It can be difficult to imagine what a concussion feels like if you have never had one. In the classroom, set up a number of stations for you and your classmates to visit. This exercise helps you to understand some of the things that might happen to the senses after a head injury.

At the first station, place a bucket or other large container filled with rice. Then put some easy-to-recognize objects deep in the rice. Wearing thick rubber gloves, reach into the rice. See if you can tell what the objects are. This shows you how people with a concussion sometimes don't feel things properly.

At the second station, there should be some goggles covered with petroleum jelly. You and your classmates can take turns wearing the goggles before doing some activities. Walk around the room while wearing the goggles, try to copy things from the board, or write a note. This will give you an idea of the problems people have with their vision after a concussion.

At the third station, there should be a selection of snacks. After choosing one, taste it with your nose plugged, then write a description of the taste. You then taste the same snack again without your nose being plugged, and write another description. The differences will show you how a person with a brain injury loses their sense of taste.

At the final station, collect a math worksheet that is at your grade level. Then complete the problems while wearing headphones playing very loud music. This shows you how people with a concussion can become very sensitive to noise after their injury.

After completing all the exercises, describe to your classmates what it felt like to do these things. Were some of the tasks more difficult or upsetting than other? If so, why do you think that was? Did any of the difficulties you experienced surprise you?

CHAPTER 5

CHANGING
the Rulebook

Research into concussions and their effects is ongoing. Many organizations are working on methods of recognizing concussions and helping recovery. Some sports organizations have also made changes to improve the safety of players during games and practices.

The U.S. Soccer Federation's Recognize to Recover program is directed at supporting the safety of all soccer players of all ages. It examined the safety of youth players who hit the ball with their head. This is a soccer move called heading. It found that boys and girls under 11 years old should never head the ball in games or during practices. The program also recommended that players 12 or 13 years old should practice heading for 30 minutes or less per day, and should do no more than 15 or 20 headers per week. Soccer leagues and organizations in the United States can set their own rules about heading the ball. But they must use the minimum requirements that were determined by the Soccer Federation's study.

The NFL has made 42 rule changes since 2002 to stop dangerous tackles and prevent head and neck injuries. The NFL's Heads Up program teaches younger players how to block and tackle safely. Players are taught to lead with their shoulders rather than tackling an opponent headfirst. They also learn about concussions and helmet safety. The program is used in more than 7,000 youth and high-school programs in the United States. Players in the Head's Up program had fewer concussions and recovered more quickly from concussions. However, research is continuing to examine how effective the program has been in improving safety.

In 2016, experts in youth concussion at the Holland Bloorview Kids Rehabilitation Hospital Concussion Centre in Toronto, Canada, published *Concussion and You: A Handbook for Parents and Kids*. The book helps injured people and their families to manage their concussion and recovery, and shows how important it is for people to take recovery seriously. Canadian doctors also recently developed a new series of tests that can predict whether children with concussions will have long-term problems. These problems can include headaches, dizziness, trouble concentrating, and emotional issues such as anxiety. Predicting whether patients have a high risk of long-term effects from their injury means that doctors can prescribe, or give, treatment options that will help lessen those effects.

Recent medical research and changes in sports safety have increased awareness of how serious concussions can be. This also helps you as a sports-team player or in your daily life. You do not have to do anything you believe is unsafe. If you are playing a sport and are hit in the head, you should not be pressured to continue playing the game. You have the right to ask questions about your safety. You may question whether your equipment fits properly or is damaged in some way. You might also think that something that you and your teammates are practicing could be dangerous.

Football Safety at Schools

In the NFL, only 3 percent of concussions happen during practice. Shockingly, between 60 and 75 percent of concussions sustained by college football players happen in practice. In 2016, the Ivy League—a group of American colleges, made up of Brown, Columbia, Cornell, Dartmouth, Harvard, Pennsylvania, Princeton, and Yale—made changes to improve safety in college football. New rules banned full-contact hitting in practices during the regular season. Full-contact hitting means that players hit each other in practice. Limited full contact at practices reduced the number of hits and the number of concussions suffered by the players.

Dartmouth College in Hanover, New Hampshire, was the first Ivy League school to eliminate full-contact football practices.

60–75%

Full contact during football practices was eliminated at Dartmouth College in 2010. The rest of the Ivy League later did the same. In practices, the Dartmouth players hit against pads, tackling dummies, and a mobile virtual player. This is a remotely controlled hi-tech robot practice dummy. It moves around the field just like a real player, helping the football players to practice more safely. The mobile dummy also helps players avoid the risk of concussion that they might have if practicing with their teammates.

"At this stage in their careers, these guys know how to hit and take a hit," said Dartmouth football coach Buddy Teevens. "People look at it and say we're nuts. But it's kept my guys healthy."

Other football leagues have also decided to limit the amount of full contact in practices. The NFL now allows only 14 full-contact practices in the regular season. Football coaches across the United States also stopped using training practices, such as the Oklahoma Drill, in which the players had to butt heads. New guidelines established by the National Collegiate Athletic Association (NCAA) limit the number of football practices a team can have and the number of practices that can have full contact.

The new rules about practices have reduced the number of concussions in college football. Players also have fewer back, neck, and shoulder injuries. Based on their football programs, the Ivy League also looked at ways to reduce concussions in men's and women's hockey, soccer, and lacrosse.

BIBLIOGRAPHY

WEBSITES

brainstreams.ca/learn/injured-brain/
concussion

concussionfoundation.org/
kidshealth.org/en/kids/concussion.html#

kidshealth.org/en/teens/concussions.html

medlineplus.gov/concussion.html

medlineplus.gov/concussion.html#cat_79

www.aans.org/Patients/Neurosurgical-
Conditions-and-Treatments/Concussion

www.braininjurycanada.ca/acquired-brain-
injury/prevention-and-treatment/

www.brainline.org/people-tbi/treatment-
recovery

www.businessinsider.com/what-
happens-brain-get-concussion-football-
sports-2017-9

www.coach.ca/concussion-
awareness-s16361

www.coach.ca/nathan-s-story-p154557-
preview-1

concussionfoundation.org/story/esther-
lovett/my-story-my-legacy

concussionfoundation.org/story/simran-
kohli-wasnt-plan

www.healthlinkbc.ca/health-topics/
tp23364spec

www.livescience.com/12916-10-facts-
human-brain.html

www.mayoclinic.org/diseases-conditions/
concussion/symptoms-causes/syc-
20355594

www.nytimes.com/2016/03/02/sports/
ncaafootball/ivy-league-moves-to-
eliminate-tackling-at-practices.html

www.pinkconcussions.com

www.popsci.com/what-happens-to-football-
players-brain-during-concussion

www.sports-health.com/sports-injuries/
head-and-neck-injuries/brain-rest-and-
concussion-
recovery-children

www.webmd.com/brain/concussion-
traumatic-brain-injury-symptoms-causes-
treatments#1

VIDEOS

Mobile virtual player for football training at
Dartmouth College
https://www.youtube.com/watch?v=91vgE_
ujVHM

Concussion symptoms in children
https://www.youtube.com/
watch?v=zCCD52Pty4A

Concussions and their effects
https://www.youtube.com/
watch?v=yyRBISAfb_k

LEARNING MORE

BOOKS

Carlson Asselin, Kristine. What You Need to Know About Concussions.
  Capstone Press, 2015.

Hudson, Maryann. Concussions in Sports. Abdo Publishing Company, 2014.

Monrow Peterson, Judy. I Have a Concussion. Now What?.
  Rosen Publishing Company, 2017.

WEBSITES

The U.S. Centers for Disease Control and Prevention website has information
about how to recognize and respond to concussions and other brain injuries
and minimize the risk of injury.
  www.cdc.gov/headsup/index.html

Learn more about concussions and other brain injuries.
  brainstreams.ca/learn/injured-brain/concussion

Learn more about the effects of concussion in children.
  www.brainline.org/kids-tbi/concussion-kids

Visit the Concussion Foundation website to read more personal stories
and learn more about concussions, post-concussion syndrome, and
preventative measures.
  https://concussionfoundation.org

GLOSSARY

anxiety A disorder that involves a person being excessively worried, nervous, or uneasy. It often involves panic attacks.

axons Long, thin nerve fibers that are attached to neurons

blood vessels The tubes of living tissue that carry blood throughout the body

brain tissue The material, made up of specialized cells, that makes up the brain

central nervous system The nerve tissues that control the body's activity; in humans, the central nervous system is made up of the brain and spinal cord

cells The basic units of all living things. Human bodies are made up of trillions of cells

chemical Referring to the interactions of substances

cranium The part of the skull enclosing the brain

CT or CAT scan Stands for computed axial tomography scan. An image of the organs and tissues within a part of the body, produced by a machine that sends out X-rays while it rotates around the body

diagnosed Identified a disease according to its symptoms

MRI Stands for magnetic resonance imagine. A procedure used to produce images of the body's internal organs and tissues through the use of radio waves and magnetic fields

migraines Very severe recurring headaches

mild traumatic brain injury (mTBI) Another name for a concussion; the result of head impact or the forceful movement of one's head causing a change in mental capacity, such as confusion, or unconsciousness

nausea A feeling of sickness in the stomach causing the feeling of wanting to vomit

neurotransmitters Substances that transmit messages between nerves

nerves Bundles of fibers in the body that transmit messages to the central nervous system, and from the central nervous system to other parts of the body

nervous system The system made up of cells that conduct messages to and from the brain and spinal cord to the body's tissues and organs

neurons The cells belonging to the nervous system that conduct signals and messages to and from the brain and spinal cord

neuroplasticity The ability of the brain to change its structure and function during development and after injury

pain relievers Drugs that are used to lessen or stop pain

paramedic A person who is trained to give emergency medical care

peripheral nervous system The network of nerves that make up the nervous system, utside the brain and spinal cord

post-concussion syndrome (PCS) Symptoms that occur after a concussion

pupil The dark, circular opening in the center of the eye, which lets light in

reflexes Involuntary responses of the body or its parts to various stimuli, such as coughing in response to inhaling dust

seizures Sudden attacks of illness

slur To speak unclearly so that the words and sounds run into each other

symptoms Signs that an injury has occurred or a person is suffering from a disease

temporal lobe The part of the brain that controls parts of hearing, vision, and language. There are two temporal lobes located behind the temples.

toxins Substances that can harm the body

unconscious Not conscious, or awake

vitamins Nutrients that humans need to grow and be healthy

whiplash A sudden backward, forward, or backward and forward movement of the head, causing a head or neck injury

INDEX

About the Author

Simon Rose is the author of 14 novels, 7 writers' guides, and more than 100 nonfiction books for children and young adults. He is a university writing instructor and provides editing and consulting services, writing workshops for children and young adults, programs for schools and libraries, and copywriting services for business. Learn more about Simon and his work at www.simon-rose.com.